APOLLO 11 Q&A

APOLLO 11

Q&A

175+ Fascinating Facts for Kids

KELLY MILNER HALLS

ROCKRIDGE
PRESS

This book is dedicated to my father, William E. Milner, who helped send American astronauts to the Moon.

- -

Series Designer: Diana Haas
Interior and Cover Designer: Erik Jacobsen
Art Producer: Megan Baggott
Editors: Alyson Penn and Eliza Kirby
Production Editor: Holland Baker
Production Manager: Martin Worthington

Cover photo ©NASA/Science Source. Courtesy of NASA, 2, 7, 8, 11, 14, 16, 18, 19, 21, 23, 28, 30, 32, 34, 36, 40, 42, 46, 48, 50, 52, 56, 58, 64, 66, 68, 70; NASA Image Collection/Alamy, 5; Greg Taylor/Alamy, 24; Independent Picture Service/Alamy, 26; Heritage Image Partnership Ltd/Alamy, 38; Maurice Savage/Alamy, 44; NASA/Science Source, 54; Dipper Historic/Alamy, 61; Media Punch Inc/Alamy, 63. Author photo courtesy Roxyanne Young

Paperback ISBN: 978-1-64876-591-9 | eBook ISBN: 978-1-63807-613-1
R0

INTRODUCTION

After World War II, the United States of America and the Soviet Union (USSR) were the world's leading "superpowers." They rivaled each other in space exploration and competed to prove which country was the strongest. The Space Race began when the USSR put the first satellite and the first person into space. American president John F. Kennedy challenged the National Aeronautics and Space Administration (NASA) to put the first person on the Moon. That dream began to come true on July 16, 1969, with the launch of *Apollo 11*. It required many incredible people, hard work, and scientific breakthroughs.

Got questions about the first walk on the Moon? This book will answer them and reveal things you never imagined. If you wonder what a word in **bold** means, check the glossary at the back of book to find out.

Prepare to explore the amazing Apollo 11 mission. It's out of this world!

JOURNEY TO SPACE

TRUE OR FALSE?

The United States of America sent the first person into space.

FALSE.

Russian **cosmonaut** *Yuri Gagarin was launched into space on April 12, 1961. He completed one* **orbit** *around Earth in his spacecraft in 108 minutes.*

The Moon from planet Earth

Twenty-three days later, NASA astronaut Alan Shepard became the first American in space.

- -

Q Why did President Kennedy challenge NASA to send a person to the Moon in 1961?

A The USSR launched the first satellite, called *Sputnik*, and the first person into space. Kennedy knew America was losing the Space Race, so he wanted America to reach the Moon first.

Q What was
Project Mercury?

A Project Mercury was a NASA program that ran from 1958 to 1963. It was America's first attempt at sending people into space to orbit Earth. That goal was achieved on February 20, 1962.

STAT: Project Mercury launched six flights with a total flight time of **53 hours, 55 minutes, and 27 seconds**.

Q What was the
Gemini Project?

A The Gemini Project helped NASA learn what astronauts could do in orbit. It proved astronauts could journey outside the spacecraft to make repairs. They could also survive for up to two weeks in space.

STAT: Gemini launched **19 rockets** into space. Two were test missions, and seven were missions to prove two ships could **dock** in space. These first missions did not have people on board. The last 10 missions carried two astronauts into orbit around Earth.

TRUE OR FALSE?

*Space suits for the Mercury and Gemini missions did not have **life support systems**.*

TRUE.

Pioneering astronauts were never outside their spacecraft, so they didn't need portable life support. But when people started taking spacewalks, the space suits had to improve.

- -

Q **What does EVA stand for during a space mission?**

A **EVA is short for extravehicular activity. It's when astronauts go outside their spacecraft.**

TRUE OR FALSE?

Americans performed the first EVA.

FALSE.

Russian cosmonaut Alexei Leonov took the first spacewalk on March 18, 1965, during his country's Voskhod 2 mission.

- -

Did You Know?

The first American EVA was performed by Edward H. White II on June 3, 1965, during the Gemini 4 mission. He wore a special space suit and a visor lined with gold. The visor protected his eyes from unfiltered sunlight.

SUITING UP!

Q When were the first space suits created?

A In 1959, scientists at tire company B.F. Goodrich were hired to develop a pressure suit for Project Mercury. NASA paid them $98,000 to make 21 suits. The suits were designed to protect astronauts if the ship's life support failed.

Mercury space suit

Q When were the space suits delivered?

A By January 1960, 10 pressure suits were delivered to NASA for training. Several problems were discovered, and the suit was adjusted to improve an astronaut's ability to move.

Did You Know?

The Mercury space suit was an updated version of a suit worn by pilots.

STAT: The first Mercury pressure suits weighed **22 pounds** (10 kilograms) on Earth. They were weightless in space.

Did You Know?

Every pressure suit was specially fitted to an individual astronaut. Each astronaut had three suits—one for training, one for space flights, and one for backup.

Q What did the first Russian cosmonaut wear in space?

A Yuri Gagarin wore an orange SK-1 pressure suit in 1961. It had an inflatable rubber collar in case his **capsule** landed in the ocean. There was a mirror sewn into the sleeve so he could see more switches and **gauges** in the spacecraft. It also had leather gloves, leather boots, and a leather radio headset.

Did You Know?

The first space suits included medical equipment to keep track of the astronauts' body temperatures, breathing rates, and heart rates. Doctors monitored them on Earth.

Mercury's "Original Seven" astronauts

Q What were the pressure suits made of?

A Each suit had an inner layer made of a material called **neoprene**. It was coated with a nylon fabric. This helped control the astronaut's body temperature. The outer layer was heat-reflective aluminum nylon fabric. The helmet attached to the suit with a metal neck ring. Straps could adjust the fit of the suit to prevent it ballooning in space. Mercury astronauts never had to use the emergency life support.

STAT: Each Mercury pressure suit had 13 zippers to guarantee a good fit.

Q How important were Mercury pressure suit helmets?

A They were essential. Each helmet had a clear visor, earphones to hear instructions from ground control, and microphones so the astronaut could answer. When the suits were plugged into the spacecraft, fresh oxygen was pumped into the helmet. A hose near the right ear removed body odor, carbon dioxide, and stray astronaut hairs.

Q How did scientists improve the pressure suit between the first and last Mercury missions?

A Tiny flashlights were added to make capsule buttons and gauges easier to see. The wrist seals were also adjusted, and a urine-collection device was installed.

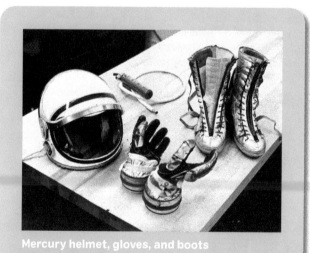

Mercury helmet, gloves, and boots

THE WALKABOUT

TRUE OR FALSE?

Before astronauts first walked in space, their space suits had to be updated.

TRUE.

To step out of the capsule, astronauts needed new protections. They required longer breathing tubes and a superstrong **tether** *to keep them from drifting off into space. They also needed special gloves to protect their hands from subzero temperatures.*

- -

Did You Know?

Astronaut Ed White's spacewalk lasted 23 minutes. White said leaving the capsule was the scariest part of the mission. He also said ending the spacewalk was the saddest moment of his life.

Q Was walking in space the only new achievement during the Gemini missions?

A No. Gemini astronauts also perfected docking, or the manual joining of two spacecraft, in space. That skill was essential to landing on the Moon, so it was a gigantic achievement.

FLY ME TO THE MOON

STAT: The Apollo program's goal was to send people to the Moon. **Twelve** missions helped achieve that goal. *Apollo 11* was the first to land on the Moon. **Five** more teams also landed.

Q How did NASA take astronauts from space to the surface of the Moon?

A In the Apollo missions, two spacecraft had to launch together—the Command Service Module and the Lunar Module. They also had to separate from each other in space. The Lunar Module would land on the Moon, then later rejoin the Command Service Module for the trip back to Earth.

STAT: On each successful Apollo mission, the Command Service Module and its pilot orbited **47,400 feet** (14,447 meters) above the Moon. The Lunar Module carried two other astronauts to the surface.

Did You Know?

Apollo 13 suffered a **malfunction** and had to return to Earth without landing on the Moon.

Apollo mission patch

STAT: **Thirty-one** astronauts participated in the Apollo program. Only **28** survived the dangerous missions.

TRUE OR FALSE?

Three astronauts scheduled to fly on Apollo 1 *were killed in a tragic fire.*

TRUE.

On January 27, 1967, Gus Grissom, Ed White, and Roger Chaffee were preparing for their final launch on the Apollo 1 *launchpad in Florida. A spark caused the pure oxygen they were breathing to catch fire. In a flash, the crew was lost. After the accident, NASA made all capsules fireproof.*

Did You Know?

The Apollo 1 mission was originally called Apollo Saturn-204 before it was renamed.

Q What propelled the astronauts, the Command Service Module, and the Lunar Module into space?

A The Saturn IB rocket carried astronauts into space during Apollo test missions. It was as tall as a 22-story building. The rest of the Apollo flights were launched by the powerful Saturn V rocket. It was about as tall as a 36-story building and made it possible for people to walk on the Moon.

Did You Know?

Mercury and Gemini capsules had room for one and two astronauts, respectively. Apollo had room for three. The Lunar Module carried two.

Q Why did it take three different space programs to get to the Moon?

A Each program taught us something new about space travel. Mercury taught us how to orbit Earth. Gemini taught us how to dock. Apollo taught us how to get to the Moon and back. When astronauts go to Mars, it will be thanks to Mercury, Gemini, and Apollo.

FAMOUS MERCURY, GEMINI, AND APOLLO ASTRONAUTS

ASTRONAUT	MISSION
Edwin E. "Buzz" Aldrin Jr.	Gemini 12, Apollo 11
Neil A. Armstrong	Gemini 8, Apollo 11
Frank Borman	Gemini 7, Apollo 8
Roger B. Chaffee	Apollo 1
Michael Collins	Gemini 10, Apollo 11
Richard F. Gordon Jr.	Gemini 11, Apollo 12
Virgil I. "Gus" Grissom	Mercury 4, Gemini 3, Apollo 1
James B. Irwin	Apollo 15
James A. Lovell Jr.	Gemini 7, Gemini 12, Apollo 8, Apollo 13
Walter M. Schirra Jr.	Mercury 8, Gemini 6-A, Apollo 7
Alan B. Shepard Jr.	Mercury 3, Apollo 14
Edward H. White II	Gemini 4, Apollo 1

THE APOLLO 11 CREW

Apollo 11 flight crew

Q Why was Neil A. Armstrong chosen to command *Apollo 11*?

A Armstrong was a fighter pilot in the US Navy. He flew 78 combat missions, then joined the National Advisory Committee for Aeronautics (NACA) as a test pilot. When NACA became NASA, Armstrong tested aircraft that flew 4,000 miles per hour (6,400 kilometers per hour). After mastering 200 different aircraft, Armstrong became an astronaut. His experience made him the perfect commander of *Apollo 11*.

Did You Know?

Armstrong received the Presidential Medal of Freedom, the Congressional Gold Medal, the Congressional Space Medal of Honor, and the NASA Distinguished Service Medal.

Q Why was Michael Collins chosen to pilot the Command Module for *Apollo 11*?

A Collins joined the Air Force as a test pilot. In four years, he logged 4,200 hours testing airplanes. NASA recruited him in 1963. He piloted *Gemini 10* for a three-day space mission.

TRUE OR FALSE?

Michael Collins became director of the National Air and Space Museum in 1971.

TRUE.

Eight million people visit the museum in Washington, DC, each year.

- -

Q Why was Edwin E. "Buzz" Aldrin Jr. chosen to pilot the Lunar Module?

A Buzz Aldrin earned a doctorate of science in astronautics at the Massachusetts Institute of Technology. He pioneered underwater training as a way to simulate weightlessness in space.

TRUE OR FALSE?

Buzz Aldrin saw a UFO in space.

TRUE.

Aldrin saw an unidentified object, but it was likely a panel that had detached from their spacecraft.

- -

WHAT ABOUT THE ROCKET?

TRUE OR FALSE?

In 1969, Saturn V was the biggest, most powerful rocket made in the United States.

TRUE.

Saturn V was designed by Dr. Wernher von Braun at NASA's Marshall Space Flight Center in Huntsville, Alabama.

Vehicle Assembly Building

STAT: Saturn V was **363 feet** (110 meters) tall and weighed **6.1 million pounds** (2.8 million kilograms).

Q Where was Saturn V built?

A The rocket was built at the Vehicle Assembly Building (VAB) at NASA's Kennedy Space Center in Florida.

STAT: The VAB is **525 feet** (160 meters) tall and **518 feet** (158 meters) wide. It is made of **65,000 cubic yards** of concrete and **98,590 tons** of steel.

Q How was the rocket moved from the VAB to the launchpad?

A A pair of flat vehicles called "crawlers" carried Saturn V.

STAT: The crawlers were the size of a baseball infield and weighed **6.6 million pounds** (3 million kilograms). They could carry **18 million pounds** (8 million kilograms). They moved at about **1 mile per hour** (1.6 kilometers per hour) when fully loaded.

TRUE OR FALSE?

The F-1 engine was the most powerful rocket engine ever built at the time.

TRUE.

*Saturn V's five F-1 engines provided 7.5 million pounds (3.4 million kilograms) of **thrust** as the rocket lifted off.*

- -

Q What kind of rocket fuel launched the Saturn V rocket?

A Saturn V was a three-stage rocket with three phases of thrust to carry the astronauts into space. The first stage burned kerosene and liquid oxygen. The second stage burned liquid hydrogen fuel mixed with liquid oxygen. The third stage burned liquid hydrogen and liquid oxygen.

MISSION CONTROL

Q What was the MOCR?

A The Mission Operations Control Room (MOCR) handled all aspects of the mission from an auditorium in Houston, Texas. The scientists in the MOCR worked hard to solve problems that could endanger missions.

The MOCR in Houston, Texas

Did You Know?

Dozens of people also worked at Launch Control in Florida. They handled liftoff and could watch the Saturn V a few miles away.

TRUE OR FALSE?

Only one woman worked in the Florida Launch Control room when Apollo 11 *took off.*

TRUE.

JoAnn Morgan was a firing room instrumentation controller. She was the first woman to be considered an official NASA launch team member.

MORE APOLLO WOMEN

Q Who was
Margaret Hamilton?

A Margaret Hamilton was the director of
the Software Engineering Division at
the Massachusetts Institute of Technology's
Instrumentation Laboratory. She helped write the
computer programs for *Apollo 11*, something that had
never been done before.

Q Who was
Katherine Johnson?

A Katherine Johnson was an aerospace technologist
for NASA. As a math whiz, she made calculations
that guaranteed that the Apollo astronauts would
make it safely to the Moon and back. The movie *Hidden
Figures* was based on her life.

Katherine Johnson—human computer

Q Who was Judy Sullivan?

A As the lead engineer for the biomedical system, Judy Sullivan monitored Armstrong's health during his trip to the Moon and back.

Q Who was Mary Jackson?

A Mary Jackson was NASA's first Black female aeronautical engineer. She studied the impact of **supersonic** speed on spacecraft.

STAT: In 1972, only **16.2 percent** of the entire NASA workforce were women.

TRUE OR FALSE?

Only 65 of the 566 people who have gone to space have been female.

TRUE.

Organizations like Space4Women are trying to change that by keeping girls engaged in science education.

- -

Did You Know?

The first woman in space was Russian cosmonaut Valentina Vladimirovna Tereshkova. She circled Earth 48 times.

ASTRONAUT TRAINING CAMP

Astronauts training underwater

TRUE OR FALSE?

To become an astronaut, you only need to go to college.

FALSE.

Once an astronaut is accepted by NASA as a pilot or a mission specialist, training begins. Astronauts learn how to work in space by practicing on Earth.

- -

Did You Know?

The first astronauts were selected in 1959. More than 321 candidates have been chosen since then. They train at the Johnson Space Center in Houston, Texas. Many have backgrounds in engineering, science, and the military.

Q What do astronauts learn in the Neutral Buoyancy Laboratory?

A Astronauts practice in models of space vehicles inside a huge swimming pool. They spend up to seven hours a day underwater, practically weightless, to prepare for orbit.

STAT: The Neutral Buoyancy Laboratory pool is filled with **6.2 million gallons** (23.4 million liters) of water. It is a little longer and a lot wider than an Olympic-size pool—and six times deeper.

Q What is the KC-135?

A The KC-135 is an airplane used to simulate zero gravity. The plane flies to 32,000 feet (9,800 meters), then suddenly dives to 24,000 feet (7,300 meters), like a roller coaster. For 25 seconds, people inside feel weightless. They repeat the process 30 times to prepare for space. The KC-135 has been nicknamed the "Vomit Comet" because it makes many astronauts sick to their stomachs.

Did You Know?

Space sickness happens because zero gravity confuses the inner ear, which makes astronauts dizzy.

Q What is the Air Bearing Floor?

NASA's Earth Fleet

A Moving a heavy object in space is easy because it doesn't feel heavy. But heavy things can break equipment inside a spacecraft if pushed too hard. Astronauts practice control and precision on the Air Bearing Floor. It's like a giant air-hockey table.

Q How long do astronauts train before going into space?

A Astronauts have to finish two years of NASA training before their first missions.

Q Can you work for NASA without going to space?

A Yes! NASA hires specialists in many fields. In 2019, 66,000 people worked on solid ground as aerospace engineers.

INSIDE THE COLUMBIA

The *Apollo 11* Command Module, *Columbia*

Did You Know?

The Command Module that carried Neil Armstrong, Buzz Aldrin, and Michael Collins to the Moon was called *Columbia*.

Q What happened if something broke in the Command Module?

A Each astronaut carried a tool kit to make minor repairs. It included 11 different tools, such as a standard wrench and screwdrivers. There was also "Tool B," an emergency L-wrench that could apply great force if anything got stuck.

Q How much room did the astronauts have inside *Columbia*?

A *Columbia* was about the size of a large car. It was the main living and working quarters.

Q What happened if an astronaut got hurt?

A The medical kit stored in the Command Module contained motion sickness shots, pain relief shots, first aid ointment, bandages, a thermometer, eye drops, nasal spray, antibiotics, decongestants, anti-diarrheal medication, and aspirin.

Did You Know?

The seats in the Command Module were called couches because they were slightly reclined inside the capsule.

Q What did the astronauts have to monitor in the Command Module?

A There were dozens of gizmos in front of the astronauts, including the Stabilization and Control System (SCS). The SCS controls a spacecraft's "attitude." That means the direction it is moving in zero-gravity space, where left, right, up, and down are hard to see.

SPACE FOOD AND FUN

Did You Know?

Apollo missions were the first space missions to have hot water.

Q What did astronauts eat on *Apollo 11*?

A The food on Mercury and Gemini missions was terrible, but *Apollo 11* meals were new and improved. By mixing hot water with dehydrated food in sealed pouches, the astronauts were able to eat things like beef and vegetables, pork with scalloped potatoes, and Canadian bacon with applesauce.

You can buy astronaut ice cream at space museums

STAT: Astronauts consumed 2,800 calories each day in space—that's 600 more calories than they would need sitting still on Earth. But Neil Armstrong still lost almost 9 pounds (4 kilograms) during the Apollo mission.

Q What did the astronauts do for fun in the Command Module?

A They listened to music, joked with each other, read newspapers, and filmed segments for news programs back on Earth. They also searched for their favorite stars as they gazed out the capsule windows.

STAT: *Apollo 11* entered the Moon's orbit on July 19, after traveling 76 hours and 240,000 miles (386,000 kilometers) from Earth.

Did You Know?

The Lunar Module was stored in the Service Module. The *Apollo 11* astronauts had to open the Service Module, then send the Lunar Module into space as they circled the Moon. After that, the *Apollo 11* team had to dock with the Lunar Module so two astronauts could climb inside it later. The Gemini missions taught them how to do this.

THE FOUR-LEGGED MOON MODULE

Did You Know?

Columbia, the *Apollo 11* Command Module, was named after a space gun in the Jules Verne book *From the Earth to the Moon*. The Lunar Module was called *Eagle*. It was named after the bald eagle, a symbol of the United States.

Lunar Module on the Moon

TRUE OR FALSE?

The Lunar Module was once called the Lunar Excursion Module.

TRUE.

"Excursion" means a short journey. Armstrong and Aldrin were only going to be on the Moon for a short time. But NASA thought the word "excursion" made the Lunar Module sound unimportant. Because it was a very serious piece of equipment, they changed the name.

Did You Know?

The Lunar Module was about half the size of the Command Module.

STAT: The Lunar Module was **17.9 feet** (5.4 meters) tall and about **14 feet** (4.3 meters) in diameter. The four-legged landing gear it used to touch down stretched across **29.75 feet** (9.07 meters).

Q Why did the Lunar Module have four legs?

A Engineers decided four legs would make the Lunar Module nice and steady when it touched down on the Moon. They were right.

Did You Know?

There was very little room in the Lunar Module, so the astronauts had to stand while they were inside it.

Q Was *Apollo 11* the only spacecraft with a Lunar Module?

A No. The Lunar Module was tested in Earth's orbit by *Apollo 9*. It was tested in the Moon's orbit by *Apollo 10*. Six more Lunar Modules landed on the Moon.

MOON BUGGY IN MOTION

TRUE OR FALSE?

The Lunar Module could fly on Earth, too.

FALSE.

The Lunar Module was the most reliable part of the Apollo missions, but it was not built to fly in Earth's atmosphere.

- - - - - - - - - - - - - -

Moon buggies expanded astronaut reach

Did You Know?

Three Lunar Modules—on *Apollo 15*, *16*, and *17*—carried Lunar **Rover** Vehicles (LRVs) to the surface of the Moon. LRVs were nicknamed "moon buggies." They allowed astronauts to explore more of the Moon's surface.

Q Who built the LRV?

A Chrysler wanted to build the LRV, but Boeing won the contract. Their moon buggy could run in extreme temperatures.

Q How did NASA fit a moon buggy inside the Lunar Module?

A Technicians who created the moon buggy designed it to fold in three places. Even the wheels folded up to make it smaller.

Q How did the astronauts steer the Lunar Rover Vehicle?

A A T-shaped joystick between the LRV's two seats made it possible to control the vehicle. When the astronauts pushed the joystick forward, the LRV went forward. When the joystick was pushed to the right or left, the rover went right or left. To stop the rover, they pulled backward on the joystick. To do all of this in reverse, they switched a toggle, and back they went.

Did You Know?

The LRV did not need rubber tires. The wheels were covered in a special **mesh** that helped the LRV roll over the fine dust covering the surface of the Moon.

EXPLORING THE EAGLE

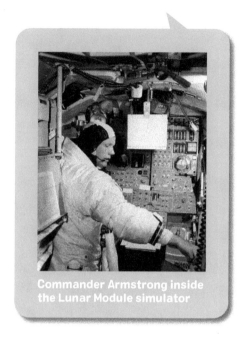

Commander Armstrong inside the Lunar Module simulator

Did You Know?

There was a Lunar Module simulator for astronaut training at the Kennedy Space Center in Merritt Island, Florida.

Q Why did parts of the Lunar Module look gold?

A Those parts were covered in gold Mylar, which is the same material as shiny birthday balloons. This protected the astronauts by preventing the Lunar Module from getting too hot or too cold.

Q What was inside the Lunar Module when it landed on the Moon?

A There were five storage compartments. They held the engine, a water tank, an oxygen tank, equipment for experiments, and the moon buggy.

STAT: The Lunar Module's guidance computer was smaller than most computers in 1969. It was 24 inches (60 centimeters) long, 12.5 inches (32 centimeters) wide, and 6 inches (15 centimeters) tall. It also weighed 70 pounds (32 kilograms). This was considered small at the time!

Did You Know?

Five mainframe computers in Houston, Texas, helped launch *Apollo 11*. They were called System 360 Model 75s. The machines that helped run these computers took up whole rooms—from **2,000** to **10,000 square feet** (200 to 1,000 square meters).

TRUE OR FALSE?

The company IBM created the mainframe computers at NASA.

TRUE.

IBM was an important partner to NASA. Not only did it create the mainframe computers, but it also created many of the computer programs that made them run. This helped put Apollo 11 on the Moon.

Aldrin unloads the Apollo Lunar Surface Experiments Package

Q What was the Apollo Lunar Surface Experiments Package?

A A kit on *Apollo 11* to help the astronauts perform two science experiments on the Moon. One measured moonquakes, and the other measured dust. Both were powered by the Sun.

Did You Know?

Apollo 11 put laser ranging retroreflectors on the Moon. They were 100 silica cubes attached to a panel. These space-age mirrors reflected laser beams sent from Earth back to Earth.

Q What was the Modularized Equipment Stowage Assembly?

A A set of tools to gather and store rock and soil samples from the Moon. There was also equipment to take photographs.

Did You Know?

The *Apollo 11* astronauts performed a mini experiment on the Moon. They set out a panel of aluminum foil for 1 hour and 17 minutes. It collected atomic particles called solar wind. Scientists analyzed the particles when the panel came back to Earth.

Q Why didn't the astronauts do more experiments on the Moon?

A *Apollo 11* was the very first trip to the Moon. The mission itself was an experiment, so only a few simple tests were performed on that first trip. But later Apollo missions did more experiments to help us understand the Moon and space better.

Q How did NASA take the picture of the first astronaut stepping on the Moon?

A A camera was right next to the ladder that Armstrong and Aldrin used to climb from the Lunar Module to the surface of the Moon.

LUNAR MODULE'S DESCENT

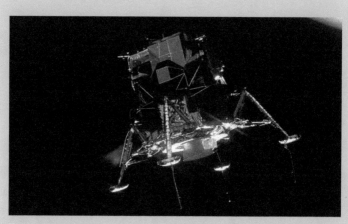

The Lunar Module prepares to land

Q When did the Lunar Module leave the Command Module and head to the Moon?

A On July 20 at 1:46 p.m., Collins said goodbye to Armstrong and Aldrin as they climbed into the Lunar Module. If everything went as planned, they would be on the Moon in just two hours.

Did You Know?

The *Apollo 11* astronauts used something called the display keyboard to talk to their Lunar Module guidance computer. They used one of 100 noun/verb combinations to ask it questions. The computer responded with numbers. The numbers in each response had different meanings.

TRUE OR FALSE?

Just before the Lunar Module touched down at 4:17 p.m., the mission was almost canceled.

TRUE.

The guidance computer flashed five warnings that nearly jeopardized the mission. It flashed because of a faulty radar antenna on the Lunar Module. It was sending too much information to the computer—information the astronauts didn't need to land. Once they figured that out, the mission continued.

- -

Did You Know?

The Lunar Module strayed off course a little and hovered over truck-size boulders. Commander Armstrong carefully steered the Lunar Module away from the rocks and landed.

Q Where did the Lunar Module land?

A It touched down in the Sea of **Tranquility**, a giant crater on the Moon. The landing spot was just a few yards away from the original location NASA had selected.

STAT: The Lunar Module had only **15 seconds** of fuel loft in ito deocont tonk when it landed.

ONE GIANT STEP: THE MOON WALK

STAT: The Sea of Tranquility is **544 miles** (876 kilometers) wide. It was a very large target.

TRUE OR FALSE?

Armstrong said, "The Eagle has landed," when he radioed ground control.

TRUE.

Ground control answered that they could finally breathe again.

- - - - - - - - - - - - - - - - - -

Q What was the first food eaten on the Moon?

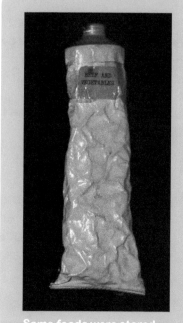

Some foods were stored in tubes, like this meal of beef and vegetables from a Mercury mission

A Armstrong and Aldrin celebrated by eating bacon cubes, peach cubes, and sugar cookie squares.

Did You Know?

Aldrin took **communion** on the Moon.

Did You Know?

The astronauts started their Moon walk five hours early at 10:39 p.m. They were too excited to wait.

Q Who set foot on the Moon first?

A Neil Armstrong climbed down the ladder first. Buzz Aldrin left the Lunar Module second.

Q What did Armstrong say as he stepped off the ladder?

A "That's one small step for man, one giant leap for mankind."

TRUE OR FALSE?

Armstrong meant to say, "That's one small step for a man, one giant leap for mankind."

TRUE.

He insisted that "a" be included, but it was recorded without it.

Q What did Buzz Aldrin say when he stepped onto the Moon?

A When Aldrin jumped off the ladder, he said, "Beautiful view. . . . Magnificent desolation."

Aldrin's footprint in moondust

STAT: The Lunar Module ladder had nine rungs, each **9 inches** (23 centimeters) apart. The gap between the last rung and the Moon was **30 inches** (76 centimeters).

Did You Know?

Neil Armstrong gathered samples of rocks and soil as soon as he set foot on the Moon.

Q How was the American flag the astronauts placed on the Moon different from a usual flag?

A There is no wind on the Moon, so engineers created a new flagpole. The flag was attached to a crossbar, so it looks like it's fluttering in the wind.

TRUE OR FALSE?

Armstrong and Aldrin took beautiful pictures on the Moon.

TRUE.

Armstrong captured his own reflection in Buzz Aldrin's helmet visor. Buzz Aldrin took a picture of his own footprint in lunar dust.

- -

Did You Know?

Gravity on the Moon is one-sixth of Earth's gravity. That means if you could jump 18 inches (46 centimeters) on Earth, you could jump 9 feet (2.7 meters) on the Moon.

Q If the *Apollo 11* astronauts had jumped too high, would they have floated out into space?

A No. There was enough gravity on the Moon to keep them safe.

Q What was Collins doing while the other two astronauts were on the Moon?

A Collins was alone for more than 21 hours, circling the Moon once every two hours. He monitored all the instruments, talked with ground control, and took in the view.

ROCK AND ROLL

Rocks on the Moon

STAT: Apollo astronauts collected **842 pounds** (382 kilograms) of rocks, pebbles, sand, and dust from the Moon between 1969 and 1972.

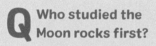

Q Who studied the Moon rocks first?

A The Lunar Receiving Laboratory in Houston, Texas, was the first to study the *Apollo 11* Moon rock samples.

Did You Know?

Many of the Moon rocks are volcanic. Moon rocks taught us that there were volcanoes on the Moon for billions of years.

TRUE OR FALSE?

Some of the volcanic Moon rocks had holes.

TRUE.

Scientists haven't figured out how it happened. Holes in volcanic rock usually occur when water or gases are heated and escape from lava. But there are no gases on the Moon, and there is no water.

- -

Q **Have there been other Moon volcano surprises?**

A **Yes. Some of the Moon volcanoes are younger than we expected. Some were still erupting when dinosaurs roamed Earth.**

Q **Could volcanoes erupt on the Moon in the future?**

A **We aren't sure. But scientists haven't ruled it out. There could be more lava under the Moon's surface. We may one day witness a lunar volcano through our telescopes.**

Did You Know?

Natural glass is rare on Earth but very common on the Moon. It is created when a meteorite strikes the Moon and melts the sand to form the glass.

THE WORLD WAS WATCHING

Mankind's most APOLLO fantastic leap to planets

Newspapers around the world told the story

STAT: In 1969, **95 percent** of all American households had television sets. Almost all of them—**93 percent**—were tuned in to watch the Moon walk.

Did You Know?

Newscaster Walter Cronkite shared an amazing fact on television. He explained that between 1900 and 1969, humans had gone from the horse and buggy to spacecraft.

Q How many people watched the Moon landing worldwide?

A Experts believe 700 million people watched. That was about one-fifth of the global population.

Q How long was the mission shown on TV?

A NASA shared 31 hours of the Apollo 11 mission with US television networks.

Did You Know?

People collected Apollo 11 souvenirs in 1969. There was everything from lapel pins to cloth patches, commemorative coins, postage stamps, and photographs.

Q Are those Apollo 11 souvenirs still popular today?

A Yes. Collectors search for Apollo 11 items and pay a lot of money for them. What they really want are rare NASA collectibles. One 12-by-8-inch (30-by-20-centimeter) cloth bag labeled "Lunar Sample Return" sold for $995 in 2015. When its new owner sent it to NASA to gather facts about its origins, she discovered Neil Armstrong had carried Moon rocks home in the bag. She sold it for $1.8 million two years later.

Q What is considered the most amazing piece of Apollo 11 memorabilia?

A An original 135-minute, unedited film of the Moon walk sold for $1.8 million at an **auction** in 2019.

TIME TO GO HOME

Earth was a beautiful sight from the Moon

Did You Know?

After their Moon walk, Armstrong and Aldrin settled in for a good night's sleep. Aldrin slept on the Lunar Module floor. Armstrong slept on the engine cover in a makeshift sling. Both slept in their space suits, because it was a chilly 61 degrees Fahrenheit (16 degrees Celsius) in the Lunar Module.

Q Did Armstrong and Aldrin have an alarm clock to wake them on July 21, 1969?

A No. Mission Control in Houston radioed to wake them. "Tranquility Base," they said, "Tranquility Base, this is Houston." When they woke, they saw Earth shining through the navigation telescope.

Q How did Armstrong and Aldrin prepare to leave the Moon?

A The astronauts checked to make sure all the switches and **circuit breakers** were in the right positions for takeoff. As they made their checks, they discovered the switch to start the engine was broken. They needed the engine to send them back to the Command Module.

Q How did they fix the broken switch?

A Aldrin thought pressing an object into the switch might work, but he didn't want to use his finger or a metal tool, because he feared the electricity might cause an injury. Then he remembered he had a pen in his pocket. The pen flipped the switch, and they ascended into orbit, waiting for the Command Module to pick them up.

Did You Know?

Neil Armstrong told Mission Control that things had gone well. He said, "The *Eagle* is back in orbit, having left Tranquility Base."

LEFT BEHIND

Retroreflectors were left behind on purpose

Q Did the astronauts leave anything on the Moon?

A Yes. They left half of the Lunar Module on the Moon. The other half headed for the Command Module.

Did You Know?

The *Apollo 11* astronauts left a metal plaque on the Moon. It said, "We came in peace for all mankind," and was signed by Armstrong, Aldrin, and Collins. It was also signed by President Richard M. Nixon, who was in office in 1969.

Q How much human waste did all the Apollo missions leave on the Moon?

A According to one report, all six Apollo missions left a total of 96 bags of human waste on the lunar surface.

Q What else is still on the Moon from *Apollo 11*?

A The retroreflector panel and other science experiment equipment were left behind to gather more information. Tools like hammers and scoops were left behind, too. The American flag stayed on the Moon. And some *Apollo 11* trash was left there, including human waste—urine and poop. It is still there today.

TRUE OR FALSE?

The Apollo 11 *astronauts left a tribute to the fallen* Apollo 1 *astronauts on the Moon.*

TRUE.

To honor Gus Grissom, Ed White, and Roger Chaffee, Armstrong and Aldrin left an Apollo 1 *embroidered cloth patch on the Moon. It was their way of taking their lost friends along with them.*

HOMEWARD BOUND

Apollo 11 landing site after the astronauts left

Q How long did Armstrong and Aldrin walk on the Moon?

A They explored the Sea of Tranquility for about two and a half hours before climbing back into the *Eagle*.

Did You Know?

Mission Control told Aldrin and Armstrong to get a little sleep at 4:25 a.m. the morning of July 21. They needed all the rest they could get for their trip back to Earth. Nine and a half hours later, their journey home began.

Did You Know?

It took the *Eagle* four hours to reach *Columbia*. The spacecraft docked at 5:35 p.m. At 7:42 p.m., *Columbia* **jettisoned** the *Eagle*.

STAT: Just after midnight on July 22, the *Apollo 11* crew engaged the "transearth injection burn." That meant their rockets fired to bring them to a speed of **3,600 miles per hour** (5,800 kilometers per hour) to escape the orbit of the Moon and head for Earth.

Q Did the astronauts sleep that night?

A They went to sleep at 4:30 a.m. as they drifted away from the Moon. Mission Control in Houston monitored their progress as the astronauts rested for eight and a half hours.

STAT: Earth's gravity took over when the spacecraft was **38,900 miles** (63,000 kilometers) from the Moon and **200,000 miles** (322,000 kilometers) from Earth.

TRUE OR FALSE?

Apollo 11 *was scheduled to **splashdown** on Earth on July 24, 1969.*

TRUE.

If all went well, the three Apollo 11 *astronauts would make the return trip in three days. And all did go well. Splashdown happened on July 24.*

BROADCAST NEWS

Neil Armstrong radios Earth on his way home

Did You Know?

On July 22 and 23, the astronauts filmed reports for TV and radio stations on Earth.

Q What did the astronauts say?

A Commander Neil Armstrong paid tribute to writer Jules Verne, who 100 years earlier had written about a fictional voyage to the Moon. The spacecraft in Verne's story took off from Florida and landed in the Pacific Ocean, just as *Apollo 11* was scheduled to do a short time later. The fantastical story had become a reality.

Q Did the astronauts say anything else that night?

A *Columbia* pilot Michael Collins said the Apollo 11 mission "may have looked, to you, simple or easy. I'd like to assure you that that has not been the case."

Q What is ham radio?

A A group of people who communicate with each other using old-fashioned radio equipment. Their radio waves travel hundreds or thousands of miles to reach other operators. "Ham" was a nickname that took root in the 1920s.

Did You Know?

Television and radio stations were not the only ones to pick up *Apollo 11* broadcasts. Amateur ham radio operators were also listening in secret, including citizen Larry Baysinger. When his antenna was positioned just right, Larry heard everything NASA said.

Q Did ham radio operators hear any secrets?

A No. Everything Larry heard was also on television. "That was kind of disappointing," he said.

A FIERY REENTRY

Reentry was a red-hot situation

TRUE OR FALSE?

To get back to Earth, the Command Module had to separate from the Service Module that held its oxygen tanks and electrical system.

TRUE.

The crew got up at 6:47 a.m. to prepare for separation. Six hours later, the Service Module was cast into space.

- -

Did You Know?

Firing the Service Module thruster rockets was supposed to push the spacecraft away from the Command Module, but they accidentally pushed it closer. That accident could have killed the *Apollo 11* astronauts, but luck was with them.

Q When did *Columbia* hit Earth's atmosphere?

A On July 24 at 12:35 p.m., *Columbia* reached the upper layers of Earth's atmosphere. It got so hot that all communication with the astronauts was impossible for four minutes.

Did You Know?

Columbia's reentry caused a sonic boom. That's when an aircraft travels faster than the speed of sound in Earth's atmosphere. The powerful sound it creates is called a sonic boom.

TRUE OR FALSE?

The Command Module's heat shield reached 500 degrees Fahrenheit (260 degrees Celsius) upon reentry.

FALSE.

*The heat shield reached 5,000 degrees Fahrenheit (2,760 degrees Celsius). The Command Module was **engulfed** in a fireball.*

NAVY SEALS TO THE RESCUE

Expert Navy swimmers save *Apollo 11* astronauts

Q Where did the *Columbia* capsule land?

A It landed 950 miles (1,529 kilometers) southwest of Honolulu, Hawaii, in the Pacific Ocean.

Q What was the USS *Hornet*?

A The *Hornet* was an aircraft carrier that served proudly during World War II. It was waiting 15 miles (24 kilometers) from *Columbia*'s location to rescue the astronauts from the sea.

Did You Know?

The USS *Hornet* picked up the *Apollo 11* astronauts on July 24, 1969.

TRUE OR FALSE?

Buzz Aldrin filmed the reentry through Columbia's *window.*

TRUE.

He used a 16mm movie camera to record the historic moment.

Q **What happened once *Columbia* hit the Pacific Ocean?**

A **Floatation devices automatically deployed to keep the capsule upright. The US Navy's Team 11 Underwater Demolition Team Swimmers approached the capsule by helicopter, dropped into the sea, and greeted the astronauts through their open hatch.**

Q **Why were members of Team 11 chosen to rescue the astronauts?**

A **They were the best swimmers in the Navy. Their commander, 25-year-old Lieutenant Clancy Hatleberg, required his team to practice recovery exercises in the sea.**

Did You Know?

Thunderstorms formed in *Columbia*'s first splashdown target zone, so the astronauts guided their spacecraft to a different location nearby.

Did You Know?

The US Navy Underwater Demolition Team Swimmers—UDT for short—were later renamed the Navy SEALs.

Q What did the astronauts say to the UDT members?

A All three astronauts reported that they were in good shape after reentry.

President Nixon greets the astronauts on the USS *Hornet*

MOON BUGS AND QUARANTINE

Did You Know?

Once they were recovered from the
sea, the astronauts were given
isolation **garments** to wear.

> **Q** Why did the astronauts need
> isolation garments?

> **A** NASA worried the astronauts might have car-
> ried dangerous bacteria with them from the
> Moon. The suits were intended to protect the world.

Did You Know?

The *Apollo 11* astronauts were also sprayed with
disinfectants when they were on the USS *Hornet*.

TRUE OR FALSE?

The Apollo 11 *astronauts were in **quarantine** for 21 days.*

TRUE.

Neil Armstrong even had his 39th birthday party in quarantine.

Q What happened during the astronauts' three-week quarantine?

A Doctors closely monitored all three men to see whether any mysterious health problems developed.

Did You Know?

Scientists wanted to protect any new life-forms that might have come to Earth on the astronauts' bodies or clothes or on the Moon specimens they collected.

TRUE OR FALSE?

The quarantine began the minute Armstrong and Aldrin closed the Lunar Module's hatch after they left the Moon.

TRUE.

That's why they had to change into special clothes before they boarded the aircraft carrier. Michael Collins had to be quarantined, too. He wasn't on the Moon, but he was with the astronauts who were, so he was possibly exposed to Moon bugs.

- -

Q Where were the astronauts quarantined?

A First in a trailer on the USS *Hornet*, then at the Lunar Receiving Laboratory in the Johnson Space Center in Houston, Texas.

THE MOON ROCKS!

GENERAL DECLARATION
(Outward/Inward)
AGRICULTURE, CUSTOMS, IMMIGRATION, AND PUBLIC HEALTH

Owner or Operator _____ NATIONAL AERONAUTICS AND SPACE ADMINISTRATION _____

Marks of Nationality and Registration _____ U.S.A. _____ Flight No. _____ APOLLO 11 _____ Date _____ JULY 24, 1969 _____

Departure from _____ MOON _____ Arrival at _____ HONOLULU, HAWAII, U.S.A. _____
(Place and Country)   (Place and Country)

FLIGHT ROUTING
("Place" Column always to list origin, every en-route stop and destination)

PLACE	TOTAL NUMBER OF CREW	NUMBER OF PASSENGERS ON THIS STAGE	CARGO
CAPE KENNEDY	COMMANDER NEIL A. ARMSTRONG		
MOON		Departure Place: Embarking NIL Through on same flight NIL	MOON ROCK AND MOON DUST SAMPLES Cargo Manifests Attached
JULY 24, 1969 HONOLULU	COLONEL EDWIN E. ALDRIN, JR.		
		Arrival Place: Disembarking NIL Through on same flight NIL	
	LT. COLONEL MICHAEL COLLINS		

Declaration of Health

Persons on board known to be suffering from illness other than airsickness or the effects of accidents, as well as those cases of illness disembarked during the flight:

NONE

Any other condition on board which may lead to the spread of disease:

TO BE DETERMINED

Details of each disinfecting or sanitary treatment (place, date, time, method) during the flight. If no disinfecting has been carried out during the flight give details of most recent disinfecting:

Signed, if required _____ Crew Member Concerned

For official use only

HONOLULU AIRPORT
Honolulu, Hawaii
ENTERED

Ernest J. Murai
Customs Inspector

I declare that all statements and particulars contained in this General Declaration, and in any supplementary forms required to be presented with this General Declaration are complete, exact and true to the best of my knowledge and that all through passengers will continue/have continued on the flight.

The customs form all three astronauts signed

Did You Know?

Like all international travelers, the *Apollo 11* astronauts had to go through customs at the airport. They had to declare anything potentially dangerous brought back to Earth.

TRUE OR FALSE?

The astronauts were late filing their customs form.

TRUE.

Normally, people declare the day they reenter the United States, but it took longer for the astronauts to get to Hawaii from their splashdown location in the Pacific Ocean.

- -

Q What did the astronauts have to declare?

A They had to declare Moon rocks, Moon dust, and other lunar samples. All three signed the form in Hawaii.

Did You Know?

After Armstrong, Aldrin, and Collins were released from quarantine, they launched a worldwide trip called the "Giant Leap" tour. They visited 24 countries in 38 days.

Q Where did they go?

A They started in Mexico City on September 29, 1969. Then they traveled to England, Belgium, Norway, the Netherlands, Iran, Thailand, Japan, India, Pakistan, Italy, and beyond.

TRUE OR FALSE?

The astronauts met Queen Elizabeth II at Buckingham Palace in England.

TRUE.

Neil Armstrong had a cold and coughed on the queen by accident.

- -

Q How did they travel around the world?

A President Nixon let them use *Air Force 2*, the military airplane normally used by the vice president of the United States. When they returned to Washington, DC, on November 5, the astronauts and their wives had dinner with the president and spent the night in the White House.

President Nixon with the astronauts at the White House

LOOKING BACK

The world celebrated Apollo 11's 50th anniversary

STAT: The Apollo 11 mission lasted 8 days, 3 hours, 18 minutes, and 35 seconds. The Apollo 11 mission cost $355 million. The entire Apollo program cost $25.4 billion—that's $152 billion in today's economy!

Q What technological inventions were created for the missions?

A Velcro and personal computers from IBM came out of the space program.

STAT: The 50th anniversary of Apollo 11 was celebrated on July 16, 2019.

Did You Know?

The space rocks collected by NASA astronauts were worth $1.1 billion. That figure was decided in court after three NASA **interns** stole Moon rocks and were captured by the FBI.

Q Are the *Apollo 11* astronauts still alive?

A Neil Armstrong passed away on August 25, 2012, at the age of 82. Michael Collins died on April 28, 2021, at the age of 90. As of 2021, **Buzz Aldrin** was the last living *Apollo 11* astronaut, at age 91.

Did You Know?

Buzz Aldrin wrote about quarantine during the COVID-19 **pandemic**. He said, "I aim to avoid catching and spreading COVID-19, so am self-quarantining. Like you, no moon rocks surround me now. Unlike when we walked on the moon and the world looked up, today I look up to Americans, pulling together to pull through."

TRUE OR FALSE?

All three Apollo 11 *astronauts wrote books about going to the Moon.*

TRUE.

They wrote First on the Moon *together in 1970. Buzz Aldrin wrote* Return to Earth *in 1973. Michael Collins wrote* Carrying the Fire *in 1974. More books followed.*

APOLLO 12 AND APOLLO 13

Pete Conrad examines *Surveyor III* on the Moon

Did You Know?

Astronauts Pete Conrad, Richard Gordon, and Alan Bean led the Apollo 12 mission on November 14, 1969. Their spacecraft was struck by lightning twice on launch.

Q Where did *Apollo 12* land on the Moon?

A It landed in an area called the Ocean of Storms. It was within walking distance of *Surveyor III*, an uncrewed spacecraft that had been sent to the Moon in 1967. They photographed it and carried instruments from *Surveyor III* back to Earth.

TRUE OR FALSE?

Apollo 13 *was almost lost in space.*

TRUE.

A faulty oxygen tank in the Service Module exploded two days into the mission, blowing a huge part of the spacecraft into space.

Did You Know?

When Commander Jim Lovell said, "Houston, we've had a problem," Mission Control knew something had gone terribly wrong.

Q How did the astronauts get home with a damaged Service Module?

A They moved into the Lunar Module, shut down the Command Module, and steered the ship manually.

Q Were the astronauts in danger?

A Yes. But NASA used science to get them home. When it was time for reentry, they went back to the Command Module, ejected the Service and Lunar Modules, and splashed down safely on April 17, 1970.

FROM THE PAST TO
THE FUTURE

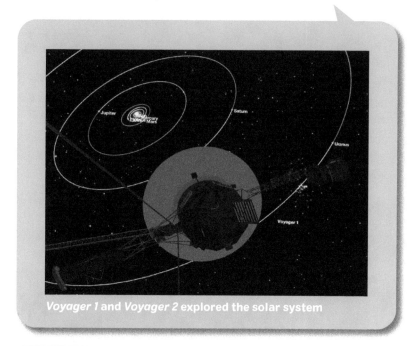

Voyager 1 and *Voyager 2* explored the solar system

Q Were there more Moon missions after *Apollo 13*?

A Yes. *Apollo 14, 15, 16,* and *17* successfully landed on the Moon and returned safely to Earth.

Q What came after the Apollo program?

A A series of test missions were followed by the launch of *Voyager 1* and *Voyager 2* in 1977. These uncrewed spacecraft were designed to explore the outer solar system. Other missions followed.

Q What did the Space Shuttles accomplish?

A The Space Shuttles did many things, including launching and repairing satellites and helping build the International Space Station.

Did You Know?

The Space Shuttle was the first reusable space-craft. And while the Space Shuttles are no longer in service, four are on permanent display at museums across the United States.

TRUE OR FALSE?

The Space Shuttle Challenger *exploded in 1986.*

TRUE.

After carrying Sally Ride, the first female American astronaut, and Guion Bluford, the first Black astronaut, into space on previous missions, Challenger *exploded on January 28. All seven crewmembers lost their lives, including the first teacher in space, Christa McAuliffe.*

IS MARS WITHIN REACH?

Mars Desert Research Station in Utah

Did You Know?

NASA's Pathfinder mission sent a **lander** and the Sojourner rover to Mars on December 4, 1996. They landed on July 4, 1997, and explored an ancient flood plain in a region called Ares Vallis. Several other rovers followed.

TRUE OR FALSE?

Missions to Mars started in 1996.

FALSE.

NASA launched Mariner 3 and 4 in November 1964. They were uncrewed spacecraft designed to fly near Mars after an eight-month journey.

Q Is the United States the only country exploring Mars?

A No. The European Space Agency, Russia, India, Japan, the United Arab Emirates, and China have all launched missions to study Mars.

Q Is it possible to send people to Mars?

A The answer is probably yes, but there are difficulties. Mars is 34 million miles (55 million kilometers) from Earth. It could take almost a year to make the journey, and another year to come home. What would the astronauts do with garbage created? Where would they live on the way to Mars? Scientists will have to figure out answers to these questions and more before we can visit.

TRUE OR FALSE?

Moon missions will help make visiting Mars possible.

TRUE.

The Moon is within reach. Testing tools and technology on the Moon will help create the tools and technology necessary to live on Mars. Living on the Moon for months at a time can teach us how the human body will react to a habitat different from Earth. Building on that first Apollo 11 Moon walk could carry us to Mars, one mission at a time.

- -

GLOSSARY

auction: a sale where buyers bid against one another to purchase items

capsule: another word for the Command Module

circuit breaker: a device that stops too much electricity from flowing to prevent equipment damage

communion: a Christian ceremony to remember the death of Jesus

computer program: a set of instructions that tells a computer what to do

cosmonaut: a Russian astronaut

deploy: put equipment into place

desolation: emptiness

dock: join together

engulf: surround or cover

garment: clothing

gauge: an electronic device used to measure information

intern: a student allowed to learn on the job

jettison: cast out

lander: a spacecraft that lands and rests on the surface of a moon or planet

life support system: a system that provides everything the human body needs to survive

malfunction: failure to perform correctly

mesh: a loosely woven material made of thread or wire

neoprene: rubber used in clothing to regulate temperature

orbit: a curved path

pandemic: a worldwide outbreak of disease

pressure suit: an inflatable suit that protects a person at high altitudes

quarantine: a time of isolation to protect people or animals from disease

rover: a person or piece of equipment that wanders

simulate: produce a copy for practice

splashdown: the act of a space capsule landing in the ocean

supersonic: beyond the normal speed of sound

tether: a rope or other connecting device that keeps a person or object contained

thrust: a strong force that moves an object forward or backward

tranquility: the state of peace or calm

Velcro: a plastic cloth that firmly grips to hold things in place

RESOURCES

BOOKS

The Fascinating Space Book for Kids by Lisa Reichley, Rockridge, 2021

Our Solar System by Lisa Reichley, Rockridge, 2020

The Story of Neil Armstrong by Sarah L. Thompson, Rockridge, 2020

MUSEUMS & HISTORICAL SITES

Smithsonian National Air and Space Museum in Washington, DC

Intrepid Sea, Air & Space Museum Complex in New York City

U.S. Space & Rocket Center in Huntsville, Alabama

Space Center Houston in Houston, Texas

WEBSITES

HubbleSite.org

NASA.gov

Space.com

ACKNOWLEDGMENTS

Huge appreciation to my father, Gene Milner, for bringing space to life for me in the past. I hope this book does the same for kids who read it in the future.

ABOUT THE AUTHOR

Kelly Milner Halls followed the Mercury, Gemini, and Apollo space missions very closely because she loved learning from her father, Gene Milner. He helped write the computer software that launched the astronauts into space. Writing this book was a labor of love for her dad, who passed away in November 2020. She felt him every step along the way, though she wishes she could have asked him thousands of questions, the way she did growing up. For more about Kelly and her nonfiction books—more than 60 of them—visit WondersOfWeird.com.

CPSIA information can be obtained
at www.ICGtesting.com
Printed in the USA
LVHW071806281221
707356LV00011B/318